READING FUNDAMENTALS

by Kathy Furgang

GRADE

3

New York

New York

An Imprint of Sterling Publishing Co., Inc.
1166 Avenue of the Americas
New York, NY 10036

ISBN 978-1-4114-7201-3

Distributed in Canada by Sterling Publishing Co., Inc.
c/o Canadian Manda Group, 664 Annette Street
Toronto, Ontario, Canada M6S 2C8
Distributed in the United Kingdom by GMC Distribution Services
Castle Place, 166 High Street, Lewes, East Sussex, England BN7 1XU

For information about custom editions, special sales, and premium and corporate purchases, please contact Sterling Special Sales at 800-805-5489 or specialsales@sterlingpublishing.com.

Manufactured in Canada

Lot #:
4 6 8 10 9 7 5 3
07/16

www.sterlingpublishing.com
www.flashkids.com

Dear Parent,

Being able to read and understand nonfiction texts is an essential skill that not only ensures success in the classroom, but also in college and beyond. Why is nonfiction reading important? For one thing, close reading of nonfiction texts helps build critical thinking skills. Another reason nonfiction reading is important is that it builds your child's background knowledge. That means your child will already have a wealth of knowledge about various subjects to build on as he or she progresses in school. You can feel good knowing you'll be laying the foundation for future success by ensuring that your child develops the necessary skills that nonfiction reading comprehension provides.

The activities in this workbook are meant for your child to be able to do on his or her own. However, you can assist your child with difficult words, ideas, and questions. Reading comprehension skills take time to develop, so patience is important. After your child has completed each activity, you can go over the answers together using the answer key provided in the back of this workbook. Provide encouragement and a sense of accomplishment to your child as you go along!

Extending reading comprehension beyond this workbook is beneficial and provides your child with the opportunity to see why this skill is so essential. You might read a newspaper article together and then discuss the main ideas, or head to the library to find a book on your child's favorite subject. Remember, reading is fun. It opens the door to imagination!

Twisters

Tornadoes are one of the most dangerous forces of nature. These huge, twisting columns of air are often called twisters. The most violent twisters can have wind speeds close to 300 miles (483 km) per hour! Even a weak tornado can ruin almost anything in its path. And to make matters worse, tornadoes can form with very little warning.

What causes these deadly storms? Tornadoes form during thunderstorms. When warm, moist air meets cool, dry air, the two hit against each other. One column of air rises up. It begins to rotate.

Most tornadoes in the United States occur during the springtime. The flat area in the middle of the United States is nicknamed Tornado Alley. Most tornadoes form here. Warm air from the Gulf of Mexico moves north over this flat ground. At the same time, cold air moves south from Canada. Twisters can form when these masses of air meet.

The United States has an average of over 1,000 tornadoes each year. Scientists use a scale from 0 to 5 to tell how strong a tornado is. More than 75 percent of these tornadoes are weak. Only about 5 percent are on the stronger part of the scale.

People can stay safe during tornadoes by following a few tips. If you hear a tornado warning on the news, move to a shelter right away. A basement is the best place to be. Go to rooms with no windows. Hide behind a hard object. This can help protect you from flying objects during high winds. A greenish sky is a sign that a tornado is coming. A roaring sound similar to a train is also a sign. If you see a tornado in the distance, seek shelter quickly. Tornadoes move very fast. Even though tornadoes can be deadly, people can do a lot to stay safe!

Read each sentence. Write *true* or *false*.

1. Tornadoes are often called twisters. _____

2. Almost all tornadoes have
   winds near 300 miles per hour. _____

3. Tornadoes form when two areas
   of warm air meet each other. _____

4. Scientists use a scale from 0 to 5 to
   tell how strong a tornado is. _____

5. Only a small percent of tornadoes
   are the strongest kind. _____

6. There are only two ways to tell if
   a tornado may be coming. _____

Superfood: The Strawberry

What's red and green and healthy all over? Strawberries! If you love strawberries, you're in luck. Strawberries love you too! The strawberry is one of the healthiest fruits around. That's because it has great benefits for the body.

One of the most important vitamins in a strawberry is vitamin C. This vitamin helps keep you healthy. It can prevent you from getting a cold. It can also help colds go away faster. The vitamin can even keep you from getting many kinds of cancers. In addition, vitamin C is great for the heart and eyes. But the super vitamin can't do its work unless it's inside your body. So eat up! Eating just one cup of strawberries gives your body 140 percent of the vitamin C it needs in a day.

Strawberries give your body more than just vitamin C. Strawberries also have potassium. This is an important nutrient. It helps muscles work and stay strong. It also helps your blood flow well through your body.

Strawberries also have a good amount of fiber in them. Fiber is important for digesting your food. It can also keep you from getting heart disease.

So why not eat a food that helps prevent diseases? In addition to being healthy, it tastes great, too. The sweet flavor of strawberries makes them taste great in many baked goods. You may have tried strawberries in muffins and snack bars. Of course they taste great on their own too. So go ahead, eat the superfood and experience the super results!

Answer the questions below.

1. What are the three main nutrients in strawberries?

_____ _____ _____

2. What kinds of diseases can eating strawberries help you avoid?

_____

3. Why is potassium important?

_____

4. According to the passage, what are three ways that someone can eat strawberries?

_____ _____ _____

5. Based on this text, what do you think a superfood is?

_____

6. What do you think of strawberries? Would you eat them more now that you know how they can help your body? Explain your answer.

_____

How to Play Lacrosse

Lacrosse is becoming one of the most popular sports in the United States. In the past ten years, it has grown 200 percent more popular! The sport is played by both boys and girls.

So, what are the rules to the game? If you have ever played soccer, you will have an easy time learning to play lacrosse.

Each game of lacrosse is split into four parts, called quarters. Each quarter lasts about 15 minutes. The two teams try to score a point. They score by getting the ball over the other team's goal line.

Teamwork is important in lacrosse. A player passes the ball by throwing it with his lacrosse stick. The next player then catches the ball. She does this by cradling the ball in the net at the end of her stick.

A lacrosse game can be filled with nonstop action. At the beginning of each quarter, teams have a face-off. Two players face each other and try to get control of the ball. When one player gets the ball, that player may pass it to a teammate. That person passes the ball again or tries to score a goal.

There are usually ten players on each team. One person is the goalie. That person stays close to the goal. The goalie tries to keep the ball from passing over the goal line. Three players are called defenders. They can stay near the goalie and help keep the other team from getting near the goal. Three other players are called midfielders. They run back and forth between each side of the field. They try to stay near the ball and get it from the other team. They also try to get the ball into the other team's goal. Three more players are called attackers. They stay on the opposite team's side of the field. They try to get the ball into the other team's goal and score. The teamwork and fast action make the game a lot of fun for everyone!

Draw a line to match each lacrosse position with its description.

1. Defender

2. Midfielder

3. Attacker

4. Goalie

a. Stays close to the goal and tries to keep the ball from passing the goal line

b. Stays near the opposite team's goal and tries to score a goal

c. Stays near his or her own goalie and keeps the other team from scoring a goal

d. Runs back and forth to try to control the ball and score a goal

5. Write in your own words how one team gets a goal in the game of lacrosse.

_____

_____

6. What is the first thing a team does at the beginning of a game?

_____

The Life of a Llama

Picture a camel. Then picture that camel without a hump on its back. Now you have a good idea of what a llama looks like! The llama is a relative of the camel. Llamas live in the wild in South America. They are very useful to the people who live in the mountains. Similar to horses, llamas carry packs on their backs for humans. A llama can carry up to 75 pounds (37.5 kg) on its back. It can then walk with its loaded packs for up to 20 miles (32.2 km) per day. Long lines of llamas move goods over the roughest parts of the Andes Mountains, along the western coast of South America.

If you give a llama too much to carry, however, you'll know about it! Llamas that have been packed too heavily will refuse to move. They'll get angry. They may spit or hiss. They may lay down on the ground. The llama is just trying to say, "I'm not going anywhere! Get this stuff off my back! It's too heavy!" Llamas are not naturally angry animals. They just know how to communicate!

Similar to their cousin the camel, llamas don't need to drink too much water. That makes them extra useful on long journeys through the mountains. They like to graze on grass. They also eat a wide variety of plants.

Llamas are such useful and smart animals that some people even keep them as pets. What would *you* do with a pet llama?

Fill in the blanks. Then answer the questions below.

1. Llamas are related to the _____ .

2. Llamas live in the wild in _____
   in the _____ Mountains.

3. Llamas can carry up to _____ pounds of goods
   up to _____ miles in a day.

4. Why shouldn't you pack too much on a llama's back?

   _____

5. What are three traits that llamas have that make them good for
   making long journeys across mountains?

   _____

   _____

   _____

6. Do you think a llama would make a good pet? Why or why not?

   _____

Old-School Video Games

Bing, bop, beep, bong! These are the sounds of the first video game revolution. Today's video game players can be thankful for their glowing handheld gadgets. Video games have come a long way since your parents played them as kids. Video games were not always so easy to carry around. They didn't really look so great. And they were not as easy to play for hours and hours.

The very first video game may date farther back than you think. At the 1939 World's Fair, a special kind of early computer was on display. It allowed people to play a very simple game against the computer. The computer won 90 percent of the time.

Over the next 40 years, scientists and college students tried to invent new games. They built them to be played on televisions and on computers.

Arcades became popular places for people to play games. People played pool there. They played pinball. Then, in 1972, a company called Atari came out with a new kind of game. It was a giant box with a computer screen inside it. The player played a tennis game against the computer. The game was called Pong. It was the first arcade video game! Through the 1970s and 1980s, teens showed up at arcades with pockets full of quarters. These quarters allowed them to play the newest games. When their time ran out, they had to let the next player have a turn.

Today, kids play lifelike games on their home computers. They carry around their own game systems in their pockets. Who knows what the next generation of video games will bring!

Answer the questions below.

1. What's the order? Write *1, 2, 3, 4, 5* on the lines.

_____ Atari invented Pong.

_____ Kids carry game systems in their pockets.

_____ A computer game is introduced at the World's Fair.

_____ Kids use quarters to play their favorite arcade games.

_____ Kids visit arcades to play pool and pinball.

2. Now summarize how video games are different today from how they were in the past. Use facts from the passage to help you summarize.

_____

_____

_____

An Astronaut's Dilemma

Imagine you are an astronaut floating in space. There is not enough gravity to hold you down. You are as light as a feather. You drift into the cabin of the spaceship, as light as a speck of dust. It sounds great, doesn't it?

There are some problems to living with no gravity. How are you supposed to prepare your meals? Soup won't stay in a bowl. Meatballs float off plates. Salad drifts around the room. And falling asleep is not so easy. Who can get a good night's sleep when floating and bumping into things? Astronauts have some tricky problems to work out while they are in space.

An astronaut's meals, snacks, and drinks must be carefully planned. Before leaving Earth, each meal is given a special treatment. This keeps the food from spoiling during a long trip to space. Astronauts add water to the food later when they are ready to eat it. It can take the astronauts up to 30 minutes to rehydrate, or replace the liquids in, a meal.

Gravity even affects the smell of food! The scents float away before they reach the astronauts' noses. Food smells often make us hungry. That means that astronauts may not feel very hungry in space. So astronauts schedule regular mealtimes. This can keep their energy levels from dipping.

Sleeping is also a challenge in space. On Earth, we feel a sense of relief when we sink down onto our beds and fall asleep. The gravity feels comforting. Astronauts must try to create these conditions in space. So astronauts get some shut-eye next to a wall where they can be strapped down. This keeps the space explorers comfortable and rested. And that's important for someone exploring the great unknown!

Fill in the blanks.

1. Astronauts float in space because _____ .

2. Astronauts must take special steps to _____ and
_____ in space.

3. Special treatment is given to meals before they are taken into space
   so that the foods don't _____ .

4. Before an astronaut eats, a meal must be _____ .
   This means liquid must be added to the food.

5. One problem with sleeping in space is _____

   _____ .

6. To fix this problem, astronauts _____

   _____ .

World's Largest Dino?

When we think of huge dinosaurs, we often think of the *T. rex*. That sure was a huge creature. It weighed seven tons! But scientists recently found a dinosaur that was 11 times that size! The newly found beast is thought to be the largest animal to ever walk Earth.

The new dinosaur fossils were found in Argentina. A farmer discovered the first bones in 2011. Then scientists got to work searching for the rest of the clues the animal left from the past. They found that the dinosaur was 30 feet (9 m) tall. That's about the height of a three-story building. It was 85 feet (26 m) long. That's longer than a tennis court. And the beast weighed 130,000 pounds (59 metric tons). That's about as heavy as two M4 military tanks!

This gigantic creature is an exciting discovery for scientists. But how did other animals that lived on Earth with it 95 million years ago feel about it? Were they frightened that such a huge dinosaur would eat them as a snack? Possibly not. Scientists believe that the animal was a plant eater, not a meat eater. That's a relief for other animals! But imagine how many plants a huge animal like that would have to eat every day. That's why the forest was this animal's ideal home.

This new dinosaur is by far the largest ever found. But we can't know the real history of Earth's creatures without studying all fossil clues. Other large fossils may be found one day. Only time will tell if this new dinosaur is really the largest to have walked Earth.

Read each statement. Write *true* or *false*.

1. A farmer in Argentina discovered a new
   dinosaur fossil.
   _____

2. The dinosaur was three times larger
   than *T. rex*.
   _____

3. The fossils show the animal was as
   tall as a three-story building.
   _____

4. The animal lived nine million
   years ago.
   _____

5. The dinosaur was a ferocious
   meat eater.
   _____

6. The dinosaur was almost as long as a
   tennis court.
   _____

Penguins

It's not easy living in a place that can feel like –76 degrees Fahrenheit (–60 °C)! But if you are an emperor penguin, it is the perfect temperature.

A penguin is a bird that can't fly. The emperor penguin lives in Antarctica. If you check a map, you will see that Antarctica is the land that is farthest south. It is so cold that few humans live there.

Emperor penguins have ways to stay warm in their cold climate. The penguins stay in groups called colonies. The colony will huddle together to stay warm. This also keeps the icy winds from hitting them. The penguins in the middle of the huddle stay warmest. So the penguins take turns. After a while, the penguins on the inside will move to the outside. This gives every penguin a chance to stay warm.

Just after a female penguin lays an egg, she goes on a hunting trip. She tries to find food for her unborn chick. While she is gone, the male keeps the egg warm. It can take up to two months for the mother to return with food. Once the baby hatches, the mother keeps the baby penguin warm in a pouch. By the time summer comes, the baby penguins can begin to swim on their own and search for food. Penguins like to search for fish in the icy waters. They can dive nearly 2,000 feet (609.6 m) and stay underwater for more than 20 minutes. Penguins are tough birds!

Answer the questions below.

1. How are emperor penguins different from other birds?
   List three different things.

   _____

   _____

   _____

2. How do emperor penguins stay warm in the freezing
   temperatures of Antarctica?

   _____

3. What job does the male penguin have when the female lays an egg?

   _____

4. How does a baby penguin stay warm in Antarctica?

   _____

5. What does a penguin eat?

   _____

6. How does a penguin get its food?

   _____

Galapagos Islands

Did you know there's an amazing place in the Pacific Ocean? It's called the Galapagos Islands. These islands are home to animals that cannot be found anywhere else on Earth. They have taught scientists a lot about how living things adapt, or change, over time.

Scientists say each type of animal arrived on the island many centuries ago. They got there by floating on ocean currents. The nearest land is 575 miles (925.4 km) away, so each floated at least that far. The islands were their new home. Birds dropped seeds from other places there. Plants grew. The animals had to adapt. If they didn't, they would not survive in the new place. For example, there are several kinds of finches on the islands. These birds could only eat the plants found there. We know that each animal has tiny things that make it different from other animals. The birds with a certain beak shape lived. They used their beaks to get the food they needed. Others died. The shape of their beaks made it harder for them to get their food. As a result, only birds with the right shape of beak reproduced. Over time, the finches looked very different from the ones that first arrived on the island. The Galapagos Islands now have at least 13 types of finches. They all evolved, or changed, on the islands. They changed to meet their special needs.

People learned about the Galapagos Islands thanks to a biologist named Charles Darwin. He traveled there in 1835. He was surprised at how different some of the living things looked. This led Darwin to understand how animals change over time. He called the process survival of the fittest. The plants or animals that don't have traits that can meet their needs will die off. They will not be able to pass on their traits. So the plants and animals on the Galapagos Islands are very special—they're the fittest there!

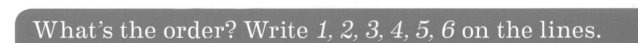

What's the order? Write *1, 2, 3, 4, 5, 6* on the lines.

_____ Seeds grew and were food for other animals.

_____ Animals floated on ocean currents.

_____ Charles Darwin arrived at the Galapagos Islands.

_____ Animals arrived at the Galapagos Islands.

_____ Animals showed new traits and began to look like a new kind of animal.

_____ Birds dropped seeds from other places.

Mount Vesuvius

Some mountains you see are just mountains. Others are volcanoes that may someday erupt with lava, ash, gases, mud, and smoke! Mount Vesuvius is a beautiful mountain near Naples, Italy. But it is also an active volcano that has had large eruptions on and off for thousands of years. It has erupted over 50 times.

The most deadly eruption that we know about happened in the year CE 79. One day, the volcano began spitting out smoke, ash, and gases. This continued for more than 24 hours. Ash rose more than 20 miles (32.2 km) into the air. The air was so thick with smoke, it could be seen miles away in the cities of Pompeii and Herculaneum.

After the ash rose high into the air, it fell heavy across the area. Several cities were buried in ash. Pompeii is the most famous of these cities. The city was buried in about ten feet of ash and mud. Two thousand people died in the disaster.

The city was lost under the ash for centuries. The buried city was not discovered until the 1700s. The discovery showed what a terrible disaster the eruption was. The hardened ash showed the city frozen in a moment in time. The forms of people were like hard fossils. Some were clutching each other in fear. The homes were left just as they were. Dishes were found on tables. Pots and kettles were found on stoves. The discovery told us a lot about the disaster. But it also told about life in ancient Pompeii.

The last time Mount Vesuvius erupted was in 1944. But one day the volcano will erupt again!

Circle the best word or phrase to complete each sentence.

1. Volcanoes are also _____.

   mountains   eruptions

2. Mount Vesuvius is a volcano in _____.

   Pompeii   Italy

3. In CE 79, Mount Vesuvius erupted for more than _____.

   a thousand years   24 hours

4. The nearby city of Pompeii was covered in _____.

   lava   ash

5. The city was lost, but it was uncovered many _____ later.

   months   centuries

6. The shapes of humans were _____ over time.

   hardened   broken up

Life Cycle of a Dragonfly

Dragonflies are amazing insects. They have two sets of wings that let them flutter above an area without moving. Then they zip away without a trace. Why haven't we ever seen tiny, baby dragonflies? That's because young dragonflies don't look at all like adult dragonflies. They go through a change called a metamorphosis.

A dragonfly lays eggs in or around water. About a week later, the eggs hatch. The animal that is born is called a nymph. At first, nymphs have no wings. They have six legs. They breathe through gills on the outside of their bodies. The gills are used to breathe, like humans use their lungs. Nymphs can live in this stage for up to four years.

Nymphs can grow for about four years. Several times during this period, the nymph sheds its outer shell, called an exoskeleton. This process is called molting. The insect sheds its old exoskeleton for a larger one.

The nymph molts up to 15 times. The last time, it comes out with its wings. At this point, the dragonfly is an adult. Dragonflies have beautiful colors, such as bright reds, blues, or purples.

Once a dragonfly becomes an adult, it lives only a short time, up to a year. During this time, the dragonflies lay eggs. This allows the life cycle to begin again.

Draw a line to match each definition with its meaning.

1. Metamorphosis   **a.** The stage of a young dragonfly

2. Nymph   **b.** A hard outer shell of an animal

3. Gills   **c.** A change that an animal goes through

4. Exoskeleton   **d.** To shed an old body part for another

5. Molt   **e.** Body part for breathing

6. Explain why we don't see tiny dragonflies that can fly around like adults.

_____

_____

_____

How to Take Great Photos

Everyone wishes they could take great photographs. Well, with a few simple tips, anyone can! Your favorite subjects to photograph might be friends, pets, family members, or flowers. Here are a few ways to think about the best way to photograph your favorite subjects.

Focus

When a photo is in focus, the picture looks crisp and clear. A photo may have some background areas that do not look focused. However, the subject should be in focus. Many cameras focus automatically. That means the camera will do the focusing for you. With other cameras, you must turn a knob or dial to make the picture look as clear as possible. It is important to know what kind of camera you have. This way you can control what the focus looks like.

Lighting

Always think about the lighting around you when you want to take a picture. You need plenty of light to take a good picture. The flash helps when you do not have enough light to take the photo. But it helps to know about your flash. They only work up to around ten feet (3 m). Anything past that point will look dark. You can use a flash inside or outside.

Framing the Shot

The frame of a photograph is the area that you see. When framing a photo, try to get as close as possible to your subject. Think about how much of the background you wish to show. Most cameras take pictures with a rectangular frame. So think about how your photo will look best. You can turn the camera sideways for some taller subjects.

Don't be afraid to tell your subjects to look at you or to move from one place to another for a better shot. You can control the pictures you take. You can make a good picture into a great picture. Then you can look back and enjoy the memories forever!

Answer the questions below.

1. Why should you know ahead of time whether your camera has an automatic focus?

_____

_____

2. Why do some photographers use a flash to take a better picture?

_____

_____

3. Why does a flash not always work for taking a better photo?

_____

_____

4. What should a photographer keep in mind when framing a photo?

_____

_____

5. What are your favorite subjects to take photos of?

_____

_____

Superfood: Carrots

When we think of carrots, we may think of them as the favorite food of rabbits or horses. But what about humans? You bet! Carrots are a favorite vegetable of kids around the world. They're crunchy and sweet. They make grown-ups happy when they see kids eating them! There are lots of different ways to eat carrots.

You may have heard that carrots are good for your eyesight. There are not many studies to show that this is true. However, there have been many studies to show that carrots are good for your heart! They can cut down your risk of getting heart disease. Even a small amount of carrots can help.

Carrots have a lot of vitamin A in them. This vitamin is great for preventing illnesses. Vitamin A also helps people get better from illnesses.

Another vitamin that is found in carrots is vitamin K. This is a group of vitamins that are similar to each other. Vitamin K keeps your bones and blood healthy.

You don't need to chomp on a raw carrot to get its benefits. You may find that you like them cooked in stews and soups. They are also great in salads. You can even enjoy carrots steamed or boiled.

Carrots are plant roots that grow underground. Just pull on the green leaves that grow above ground. The whole carrot can be pulled out of the dirt and washed before eating. You'll love eating these veggies fresh from the earth!

Read each statement. Write *fact* or *opinion*.

1. Carrots are kids' favorite vegetables. _____

2. Grown-ups love when kids eat carrots. _____

3. Carrots have vitamin A. _____

4. Carrots help prevent heart disease. _____

5. Vitamin K is good for your bones and blood. _____

6. Carrots taste great in salads. _____

Amelia Earhart

As a teenager in the early 1900s, Amelia Earhart attended a stunt flying show. She saw an airplane swoop by. At that moment, Amelia became fascinated with planes. When she took her first plane ride at age 23, she knew that she would become a pilot.

Amelia knew becoming a pilot would be a challenge. There were not many female pilots. However, she always felt that it was important to do what she loved.

Amelia did some great things during her short career in the skies. She was the first woman to fly across the Atlantic Ocean. She set that record in 1928. She and her crew were given a parade. They were celebrated at the White House. Amelia became famous.

Years later, she became the first person to fly across the Pacific Ocean. Today pilots do these things hundreds of times per day. But at the time, these were very important—and dangerous—things for pilots to do.

Amelia's next adventure would be her most dangerous of all. It would also be her last. She attempted to be the first woman to fly around the world. The trip would be 29,000 miles (46,671 km) long. She had to carry a lot of extra fuel to get her plane across wide oceans. However, a storm stood in the way of her dreams. On one of the days she took off into the skies, the weather was cloudy. It became harder and harder to see. Then, stormy weather kept her radio from working well. Her messages could not be heard. She could not hear the messages sent to her. Amelia was not heard from again.

It is still not known for sure exactly what happened to Amelia and her plane. Some researchers think the plane crashed on an island in the southwestern Pacific Ocean. However, the real story is still a mystery. Amelia remains a legendary pilot who always followed her dreams. She was the first famous female pilot. She inspired women to pursue their goals.

Read each question and circle the correct answer. Then answer the questions below.

1. When did Amelia become fascinated with airplanes?

   a) when she was a baby   b) when she went to a stunt flying show

   c) when she first rode in an airplane   d) when she flew around the world

2. Which flying record did Amelia set?

   a) first person to fly around the world   b) first person to fly over the ocean

   c) first woman to fly a plane   d) first woman to fly across the Atlantic Ocean

3. What was Amelia trying to do during her last plane adventure?

   a) be a stunt pilot   b) be the first woman to fly around the world

   c) be the first female pilot   d) land a plane in the ocean

4. What kept Amelia from reaching her goal?

   a) She became sick during her flight.   b) She decided not to take off.

   c) She disappeared during a storm.   d) Another pilot finished first.

5. Why don't we know what happened to Amelia Earhart?

   _____

6. Why were Amelia Earhart's accomplishments important?

   _____

   _____

   _____

Where Did Football Come From?

People often think of football as a very American game. It is played professionally in the United States. It is also one of the most popular sports in the country. But football has its roots in ancient Greece. A game called *harpaston* was played in Greece 2,500 years ago. The idea of the game was simple: Just stop the other team from getting a ball across the field to the other team's goal. It sounds like football, soccer, and rugby! All of these games have their roots in *harpaston.*

A game similar to the football we know today was played in England in the 1100s. But kings such as Henry IV and Henry VIII were not big fans of the game. They banned the sport so that no one could play it. They thought the game took people's attention away from sports that could help in wartime. They wanted people to practice fencing and archery instead.

The game we know as football in the United States today started as a college game. The first modern game was played in 1869 by two college teams. The rules started out similar to those of rugby and soccer. But the game of football has gone through many rule changes. Many of these changes have been to make the game safer. Changes have also been made to make the game more exciting for players and fans.

Today the game is more exciting than ever. Fans fill huge stadiums to watch football. Millions of people watch it on television. Even though it had its roots in ancient Greece, football is definitely an American sport.

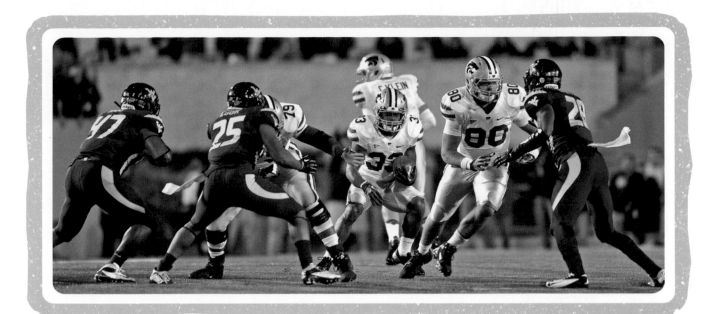

Answer the questions below.

1. Football is based on what Greek game?

_____

2. How long ago was this Greek game played?

_____

3. How was *harpaston* played?

_____

4. Why didn't Henry IV and Henry VIII let people play football?

_____

5. When did football become popular in the United States and why?

_____

6. Why do you think football is called an American sport?

_____

The Brainy Dolphin

What's that out in the ocean, jumping high out of the water? Is it a whale? Is it a shark? It's the brainiest of sea animals—the dolphin!

Dolphins are very smart marine mammals. They are found living all around the world. Dolphins live in groups. Many can live more than 40 years. There are about 40 different species of dolphins. They range in size from four feet (1.2 m) long to about 25 feet (7.6 m) long.

Dolphins are best known for being smart. In fact, they are thought to be the second smartest animal in the world. Only humans are smarter than dolphins. You may have seen dolphin smarts in action. If you have ever been to a marine park where dolphins do tricks, you have seen something extraordinary. Most other animals do not have the brainpower of dolphins. They cannot be trained to learn commands and perform a show.

Why are dolphins so smart? They are born that way. Scientists found that a dolphin's brain is big compared to the size of its body. Compared to those of other animals its size, a dolphin's brain is five times larger. This is the same reason why humans are so smart. Compared to other animals our size, a human's brain is seven times larger. This extra brain size gives animals a lot of room for thinking. They can remember small details that they learn.

Dolphins can even experience emotions. They can be sad, angry, and scared, just like humans. Scientists think the animals' smarts do more than help them just experience emotions. Dolphins can also think about their emotions. These amazing creatures are the thinkers of the sea!

Read each question and circle the correct answer. Then answer the questions below.

1. Many dolphins live to be more than _____ .

   a) 4 years old   **b)** 14 years old   **c)** 40 years old   **d)** 400 years old

2. Dolphins are thought to be smart because their brains are _____ .

   a) large compared to other animals their size

   b) larger than those of most other animals

   c) larger than those of humans

   d) designed to remember tasks

3. The only animals smarter than dolphins are _____ .

   a) dogs   **b)** whales   **c)** humans   **d)** squids

4. Unlike many other animals, dolphins can experience and think about being _____   _____ .

   a) sad   **b)** angry   **c)** scared   **d)** sad, angry, and scared

5. What makes dolphins able to perform at shows and remember long detailed tasks?

   _____

   _____

6. What is the main idea of this passage?

   _____

The United States Capitol

The founders of the United States wanted to create a special building in which laws would be made. Here, the nation's laws would be written, talked about, and passed. In 1793, they began construction. The Capitol building is where new laws are made even today.

The city of Washington, DC, had been chosen just a few years earlier to be the nation's capital. The city would be the place where the government would be run. It would be separate from any other state. The founding members of the nation then set to work. They planned to have government buildings that helped make the new nation proud.

Thomas Jefferson suggested a contest for the best design for the Capitol building. The winner would be given $500. That was a lot of money back in the 1790s! There were 17 entries, but none of them was chosen. The design was chosen later. It was created by a physician from Scotland named Dr. William Thornton.

The Capitol took years to build. When it was finished, it was the home of Congress. Lawmakers met there to discuss the nation's future. However, the building was nearly destroyed. During the War of 1812, British troops set fire to the building.

After it was rebuilt, several additions were made to the Capitol. Over the years, the building was also changed to be more modern. Electricity, telephones, and air conditioning were all important additions to the Capitol.

Today the Capitol is a great place for tourists to visit. There is a visitor center that is nearly the size of the building itself! Visitors from around the world are welcomed by the building's style and powerful appearance. The domed top looks as beautiful from a distance as it does up close.

Read each statement. Write *true* or *false*.

1. The Capitol is the place where
   laws are made and discussed. _____

2. Thomas Jefferson won a contest
   for the best design for the Capitol. _____

3. The Capitol was burned by the
   British during the War of 1812. _____

4. The building still does not have electricity,
   telephones, or air conditioning. _____

5. Visitors are not allowed
   at the Capitol. _____

6. Tourists from all around the
   world visit the Capitol. _____

Earthquake!

You feel the ground rumble below your feet. Pictures drop off walls. Books flop from shelves. Plates crash to the floor. You are experiencing an earthquake!

An earthquake can be a scary experience. It happens without warning and can be dangerous. But what causes an earthquake?

An earthquake is exactly what it sounds like. It's a quake, or shake, of the earth. This shaking happens on Earth's crust, or outer later. Most earthquakes are so small that they are not even noticed by humans. Others are sudden jolts that can be strong and violent.

Earth's crust is made of many large plates that fit together like puzzle pieces. These plates are always moving. We cannot feel most of these movements because they happen so slowly. A plate may move as little as an inch a year. But sometimes these plates may bump up against each other. One plate might move up over another. Two plates may twist or sink down. When these movements happen, the ground shakes. The bumps and hits cause waves of motion to be released. We see and feel this as shaking of the ground.

The greater the waves of energy an earthquake releases, the stronger the shaking will be. Scientists rate earthquakes on a scale of 1 to 10. An earthquake with a rating of 10 would destroy buildings and bridges. Many people could be killed. But earthquakes this large are rare. There might be one every year that is a 9 or stronger on the earthquake scale.

People have learned to live with earthquakes. Some areas get many earthquakes because they are located at the edge of two plates. Scientists have learned to make buildings in these areas extra strong. Some of the newest buildings and bridges can survive very strong earthquakes. And that's great news for everyone!

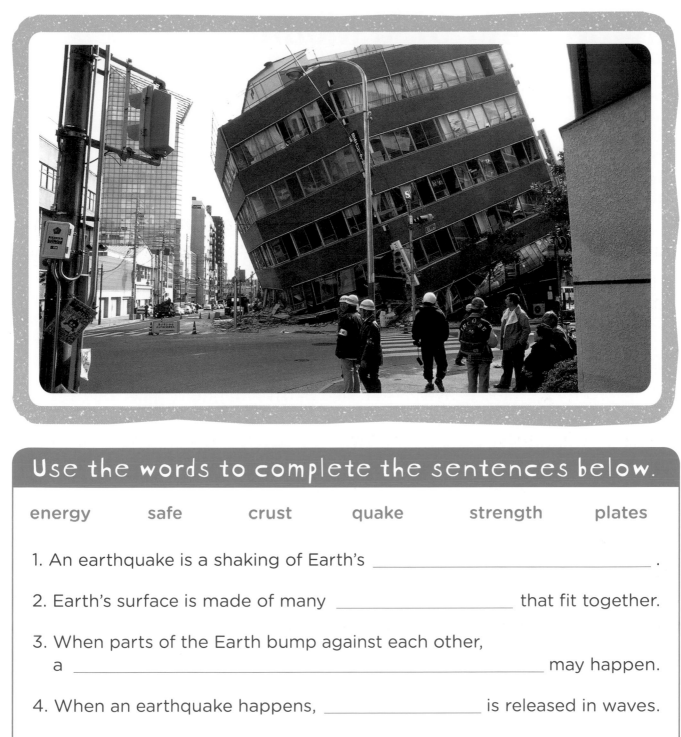

Use the words to complete the sentences below.

energy   safe   crust   quake   strength   plates

1. An earthquake is a shaking of Earth's _____ .

2. Earth's surface is made of many _____ that fit together.

3. When parts of the Earth bump against each other,
   a _____ may happen.

4. When an earthquake happens, _____ is released in waves.

5. Scientists rate the _____ of earthquakes on a scale of 1 to 10.

6. New buildings must be strong to stay _____ from
   earthquake forces.

The Making of a Mountain

Some of Earth's landforms can be made in the blink of an eye. A sandy beach can be washed away in minutes during a rough storm. An earthquake can quickly form a rocky or jagged cliff. What about mountains? Many mountains take millions of years to form. When you see a mountain off in the distance, stop and think about how that mountain formed. It may have gone through a slow process that caused the mountain to move upward. It moved foot by foot, inch by inch. Earth's plates move and crash against each other. When one moves down, the other moves up. This upward movement could be the beginning of a mountain. Over millions of years, the mountain reaches high. It adds beauty to the landscape.

However, not all mountains form the same way. Some mountains are also volcanoes. There is an opening in the earth that stretches down to Earth's middle layer. This middle layer, also called Earth's mantle, is miles below the surface. Hot magma from inside Earth might reach up out of the volcano during an eruption. This material that comes out of the mountain is called lava. Over time, lava can cool and harden into rock. Slowly, more and more lava hardens around the outside of the volcano. It becomes a mountain!

Mountains are so pretty that some people might argue that they are worth the long wait. A mountain that is forming today will be a beautiful sight for our world in the future.

Should we think only of Earth's slow processes when we look at mountains? No. Mountains can take part in fast changes also. One large volcanic eruption can blast the side right off of a mountain. Mountains can be part of both slow and fast Earth processes!

Draw a line to match each definition with its meaning.

1. Mountain

2. Volcano

3. Lava

4. Magma

5. Eruption

a. The release of materials from a volcano

b. Very hot material that flows from a volcano

c. Landform with an opening to Earth's middle layer

d. The material inside a volcano that comes from Earth's mantle

e. Landform that forms over a long period of time

6. Now explain two ways in which a mountain may form.

_____

_____

_____

How Did That Dog Get in the House?

It is said that dogs are man's best friend. But that wasn't always the case. Long ago, all dogs were wild animals, roaming free with no help from humans. Many scientists think dogs began to live with humans as pets about 10,000 years ago. Humans began to farm and produce crops for food around that time. Wild dogs may have come around looking for scraps of food from farmers. They hoped to share in the harvests. Humans and dogs slowly became friends. Some kinds of dogs became domesticated. That means they live with and depend on humans.

Why might humans have agreed to feed some hungry wild dogs? Perhaps it was because they could get something out of it, too. Dogs were good companions. They were helpful on hunting trips. They scared away other wild animals. They helped guard homes and crops. Humans saw how loyal dogs could be. Dogs had all the traits that made up a good pet.

As people began to keep their own dogs, the dogs depended on humans more and more. Today, many breeds of domesticated dogs cannot live in the wild. They depend too much on humans. But even domesticated dogs still have many traits of wild ones. They love to bury bones. They like to dig. They use their strong sense of smell to identify people and other animals.

Today, people teach dogs to fetch or roll over. But remember that when we teach a dog to beg, it's a skill they may have used more than 10,000 years ago to get close to humans. Well, the trick sure worked. Today, nearly 40 percent of households in the United States own at least one dog!

Circle the best word to complete each sentence.

1. Long ago, all dogs were _____ .

   wild   **domesticated**

2. Dogs began to live with humans around _____ years ago.

   40,000   **10,000**

3. Dogs became close to humans because they were looking for _____ .

   owners   **food**

4. Humans use dogs to help them _____ .

   hunt   **cook**

5. The word _____ means an animal depends on humans.

   wild   **domesticated**

6. Today almost _____ percent of US households have dogs.

   80   **40**

Nelson Mandela

At the southern tip of Africa lies a country called South Africa. In that country there is a tiny village that was home to one of the world's most important civil rights leaders. Nelson Mandela was born in the village of Mvezo in 1918.

Nelson was born with the name Rolihlahla. The name means "troublemaker" in his native African language. Schoolteachers began calling the boy Nelson.

As Nelson grew up, he realized that the life in South Africa was not fair. Laws kept black people and white people from living and working together. In 1948, laws were put in place that said black people must be separate from white people at all times. These laws were called apartheid.

Nelson Mandela was outspoken. He became involved in trying to end apartheid. He joined groups with other people who felt the same way.

In 1961, Nelson organized a strike. This meant that people refused to work. The strike was meant to show that people were against apartheid. They wanted it to end. Nelson and other civil rights leaders were put in jail for their bold actions. Because they were black, they were not allowed to speak out against apartheid.

Nelson spent 27 years in jail for his actions. He became known around the world for standing up for what was right. He became a hero. While he was in jail, Nelson continued to learn and grow.

Others continued Nelson's fight against apartheid while he was in jail. The unfair practice was finally ended in 1990. Nelson was released from jail. In 1991, he ran for president of the new South Africa and won. He was voted the leader of the nation. Nelson Mandela died in 2013 at the age of 95. During his life, South Africa changed a great deal. And the world saw a bold and peaceful leader in Nelson Mandela.

What's the order? Write 1, 2, 3, 4, 5, 6 on the lines.

_____ Apartheid was started in South Africa.

_____ Apartheid ended.

_____ Nelson was put in jail for organizing a strike.

_____ Nelson Mandela was born.

_____ Nelson became the president of South Africa.

_____ Nelson realized that black people were not treated fairly in South Africa.

How to Make Ice Cream

Imagine you are in the mood for some ice cream but you don't have any. Don't fret! You can make some of your own in about eight minutes. All you need is some sugar, cream, mint extract, salt, ice, and plastic bags that seal. You could be minutes away from enjoying ice cream. Here's what to do:

1. Combine a tablespoon of sugar with one-half cup of cream and one-half teaspoon of mint extract.

2. Pour the mixture into a quart-size plastic bag and seal it tightly.

3. Fill a gallon-size plastic bag halfway with ice. Add 7 tablespoons of salt to the bag and mix it around with the ice.

4. Fit the smaller bag with the sugar and cream into the ice. The ice should surround the smaller bag.

5. Seal the larger bag tightly. Shake it as hard as you can for about eight minutes. The faster you shake it, the better the results will be.

6. Remove the smaller bag. Pour the ice cream from the smaller bag into a bowl.

The ice cream will be soft, so eat it quickly before it melts! Enjoy!

Read each statement. Write *true* or *false*.

1. The ice cream recipe takes
   about five hours to make.

   _____

2. The ice cream recipe is
   made mainly of sugar and cream.

   _____

3. The recipe calls for three cups
   of sugar.

   _____

4. The ice cream is made by
   shaking the bag with ice around it.

   _____

5. You should not shake the bag too hard
   or the ingredients may not turn to ice cream.

   _____

6. The recipe can still be made
   if you leave out the ice.

   _____

Niagara Falls

At the border where the United States and Canada meet in New York State and Ontario, there's an amazing feat of nature. Niagara Falls is a giant and forceful waterfall. The waterfall formed over a very long period of time. It started when the last ice age ended about 12,500 years ago. Giant sheets of ice nearly three miles (4.8 km) thick covered the area. Then the sheets of ice melted and moved. Rivers were cut out in their paths. The Niagara River formed, along with the giant waterfall.

Niagara Falls is not the biggest waterfall in the world. About 500 other waterfalls are taller. However, the amount of water that flows over Niagara Falls is amazing. During the summer, more than 2,800 tons (2,540 t) of water move over the falls each second. That's a lot of water!

The water gets put to good use, too. Besides attracting thousands of tourists each year, the water near the falls is used for other things. It is used for drinking water, fishing, boating, and swimming. It is even used to make power.

The falls have attracted many odd tourists over the years. Some daredevils have gone over the falls. Sixteen people have tried to make the 170-foot (52 m) drop over the falls. Eleven of those people survived. Some went over the falls in a barrel to protect themselves. Others just went over with no protection at all!

If you ever visit this noisy but spectacular place, take lots of pictures. But remember to stand back!

Answer the questions below.

1. Where is Niagara Falls located?

_____

2. What does Niagara Falls have to do with the last ice age?

_____

3. How much water goes over Niagara Falls in the summer?

_____

4. How is the water from Niagara Falls used?

_____

5. What is an odd thing that some tourists have done at Niagara Falls?

_____

6. Why do you think Niagara Falls is noisy?

_____

How to Start a Recycling Program

The facts about trash are incredible. Americans throw away 25 million plastic bottles every hour. The average person makes more than four pounds (1.8 kg) of garbage each and every day. In America, enough trash was made during 2009 to circle Earth 24 times!

Trash has become a major problem. There's just not enough room to put all of our trash. Someday landfills will be full. This is why recycling is so important.

Recycling is the process of turning trash items into new items. For example, plastic water bottles can be recycled. Then they can be turned into new bottles. Did you know that about 75 percent of our trash can be recycled? But people only recycle about 30 percent of their trash. Starting a recycling program can help fix this problem.

If your school does not have a recycling program, you can help! It's easier than you think. Gather bins that can hold paper, plastic, glass, or metal. The bins should able to be moved easily. Place them around your school. Put them in classrooms, in hallways, or on the playground. Then, let people know how to use them!

Explain what the bins are used for. Include pictures of what can be recycled. Show newspapers, school paper, and cardboard. Show plastics, such as bottles and other containers. Explain that soda cans and glass bottles can also be recycled.

Have a teacher or other adult help you plan the pickup of the items. They can be sent to a recycling plant. The small efforts we put into recycling can have a great effect on our planet. Between 1990 and 2010, the recycling of paper went up nearly 90 percent!

1. Americans throw away 25 million _____ .

    a) pounds of garbage each hour

    b) pounds of garbage each day

    c) plastic bottles each hour

    d) plastic bottles each day

2. Recycling is the process of _____ .

    a) throwing trash in landfills

    b) turning trash into new items

    c) using trash again

    d) making new items

3. Which of the following items can be recycled?

    a) Earth   **b)** landfills   **c)** classrooms   **d)** cardboard

4. After people collect items that can be recycled, they are brought to a _____ .

    a) recycling plant   **b)** landfill   **c)** factory   **d)** store

5. Why is recycling important?

_____

6. What are the steps of starting a recycling program at your school?

_____

_____

_____

Could Humans Live on Mars?

Wouldn't it be great if humans could live on other planets? One of the first places humans would want to live is Mars. Humans have always been fascinated by the Red Planet. It is our closest neighbor in space. Could we live there? Absolutely not!

Mars is just too different from Earth for us to live there. There are several reasons why we are better off staying on Earth.

Temperature

Mars is about 120 degrees colder than Earth. Temperatures can get to be about –225 degrees Fahrenheit (–153 °C). That is too cold!

Atmosphere

The atmosphere on Mars does not have the same protection against the sun's rays as Earth does. So you would get a bad sunburn there!

Dust

Mars gets its nickname, the Red Planet, because of red dust in the air. This dust would be too difficult for humans to live with. Dust storms on the planet are common. The dust can be kicked 25 miles (40.2 km) into the air. This would make it hard for us to breathe.

Air

Even without all of that dust, Mars does not have enough oxygen. Humans need oxygen to breathe. This would make life on Mars impossible.

Even though humans can't survive on Mars, the planet would be beautiful to see. Mars is home to the largest mountain in the solar system. The mountain, Olympus Mons, is also a volcano. You would also see two moons when you gazed into the night sky, instead of just one. But after visiting the Red Planet, come back home right away! Conditions on Earth are perfect for humans!

Answer the questions below.

1. How does the temperature of Mars compare to the temperature of Earth?

_____

2. How does the atmosphere of Mars compare to the atmosphere of Earth?

_____

3. Why is Mars called the Red Planet?

_____

4. How would the dust on Mars affect a human?

_____

5. What would a visitor to Mars see?

_____

6. Do you think one day humans will live on Mars? Why or why not?

_____

_____

Why We Exercise

How do you feel about exercise? Some people just enjoy getting out and moving around. For others, exercise seems like a chore. But whether you like it or not, exercise is good for the body.

Exercise can fight diseases. It can help control a person's weight. Exercise can build muscles. It can help the body move more smoothly.

But exercise can do even more. You may feel tired or out of breath after you exercise, but notice what happens next. Exercise gives you energy. Your mood becomes better. This may be because the faster pumping of your heart is helping to pump more blood and oxygen around your body. Your body actually begins to work better.

And you don't need to exercise for an hour each day to get these benefits. Kids who simply get outside and run around can see the benefits of exercise very quickly. Riding a bike strengthens leg muscles. It helps the body to become more coordinated. Jumping rope or playing soccer does this too.

People who exercise may sleep better than those who don't. And that's good news for young people. When your body is still growing, you need extra sleep to stay healthy and strong.

When you mix exercise with eating a healthy diet, you will be in even better shape. When you build muscles during exercise, a good diet can keep those muscles healthy and strong. So get out there and move around! Your body will thank you.

Circle the best word to complete each sentence.

1. Humans can help fight diseases by _____ .

    working   exercising

2. Exercise can improve our _____ .

    mood   grades

3. Exercise makes the heart pump more blood and _____ .

    food   oxygen

4. Young people need more _____ than older people to stay healthy.

    sleep   books

5. Exercise improves a person's heart, lungs, and _____ .

    muscles   teeth

6. In addition to exercise, people need to eat _____ foods to stay healthy.

    salty   healthy

Spiders

Eek! A spider! Why do spiders appear so creepy to humans? Could it be their eight long legs? Could it be their round bodies, sharp fangs, or extra eyes? Whatever it is, humans tend to stay away from spiders and let them do their own thing.

And that thing that spiders do is capture bugs. Almost all types of spiders have venom. Spider venom is a poisonous liquid. When a spider bites, its venom goes into the body of its prey. Spiders mainly catch and eat insects. Often the prey will not be able to escape after it has been bitten. This makes it easier for the spider to wrap up the wiggly bug.

What happens next? The spider's body makes silk. It works like a long rope for tying up prey. Then the spider can save the bug in its web for later snacks and meals.

There are plenty of spiders around the world. There are about 40,000 known kinds of spiders. Spiders can be found on every continent except Antarctica. Some female spiders may lay up to 3,000 eggs at a time. Many spiders protect their eggs by covering them with silk.

Most spiders are not dangerous to humans. But some of them can be. The black widow spider has venom that is very toxic to humans. Bites from these spiders are very rare, though. A special medicine can help humans recover from this kind of spider bite.

Whether you love spiders or hate them, they are amazing creatures. Just watch them spin a web or catch a meal!

Read each statement. Write *true* or *false*.

1. Spiders have six legs. _____

2. Every spider has venom. _____

3. Spiders use venom to catch prey. _____

4. Once a spider catches prey, it eats it right away. _____

5. There are no spiders in Antarctica. _____

6. Humans can receive medicine
   if bitten by a black widow spider. _____

The Future of Video Games

When we think of how far video games have come, we think about how great the picture looks. Video games used to look like blips of light blinking across the screen. Today they look as real as a movie. But what does the future hold for video games? How will video games change? Many gaming companies are already working on the next big advancement in the video-game world.

Put down that controller. Soon, wearable controllers will be more popular. Placing a device over your eyes will help bring the game all around you. You can become part of the action. This kind of technology is already being tested.

In the future, you may also see video games that enter the room with you. Instead of joining the world inside your television, the opposite may occur. The game may project out of the console and into your living room. A world may appear around you that you can interact with.

And forget those buttons and switches you deal with today. In the future, you may be able to just reach out and interact with the game. You may slide images by moving your finger without even touching them!

You may have seen some of these futuristic technologies in the movies. Very often, life imitates entertainment. First, people think of the ideas. Then, scientists can work on making them a reality. Stay tuned for the next generation of video games. They may be much closer than you think!

Answer the questions below.

1. How have video games changed from how they used to be?

_____

2. How might you be able to wear a video-game controller in the future?

_____

3. How can a video game make an image appear around you in your living room?

_____

4. How might controllers change in the future so there are no buttons or switches?

_____

5. Where do some ideas for futuristic technologies come from?

_____

6. How would you like video games to change in the future?

_____

Pocahontas

Of all the Native Americans who have been part of the story of America, Pocahontas is one of the most interesting characters.

In 1607, Captain John Smith and 100 other settlers arrived in the New World. They set to work on building a colony for England. They would call the colony Jamestown.

The colonists did not always get along with the Native Americans in the area. Pocahontas was the daughter of an important Native American chief. After John Smith was captured by the tribe, he was about to be put to death. That's when Pocahontas did something that would be remembered forever. Stories say that Pocahontas saved John Smith by throwing herself between him and his attackers. To keep from killing Pocahontas, John Smith was saved. Pocahontas wanted the tribes and colonists to get along.

Pocahontas helped the Jamestown colony in many ways. She taught them about the land. She brought them food during a difficult winter. Without her deliveries of food, it is thought that the colony may not have survived.

Years later, Pocahontas married an Englishman named John Rolfe. She moved to England. She changed her name to Rebecca Rolfe. She lived the life of a European. Pocahontas always missed her life with the Native American tribes, however. On her return trip to Virginia, Pocahontas became ill. She died in 1617.

Over the years, the stories of Pocahontas have become like legends. She is perhaps one of the most famous Native Americans in history. The settlers at Jamestown had great respect for her and others like her. Many Native Americans helped the settlers survive in a harsh new land.

What's the order? Write 1, 2, 3, 4, 5, 6 on the lines.

_____ Pocahontas brought food to the Jamestown settlers.

_____ Captain John Smith and other settlers arrived in the New World.

_____ Pocahontas changed her name to Rebecca Rolfe and moved to England.

_____ Pocahontas saved John Smith's life.

_____ Pocahontas married an Englishman named John Rolfe.

_____ John Smith was captured by Native American tribes.

The Most Popular Sport in the World

If you could ask everyone in the world to name their favorite sport, what do you think the winner would be? Many people like baseball and football. Some people enjoy tennis or basketball. But there are far more soccer fans around the world than fans of any other game. Soccer is by far the most popular sport in the world!

A worldwide soccer tournament called the World Cup is played every four years. The players who play in them are very skilled. The finals for these games are played over a period of one month. Lots of people watch the World Cup. In 2014, it is estimated that around one billion people worldwide watched at least part of the final game. That's a lot of soccer fans!

Soccer is also played for fun by kids all around the world. They play in streets and on fields. They play the game all year long. Why is soccer so popular? Perhaps it is because it is so fun to play. All that is needed to play is a ball and some friends.

The idea of the game is simple. Just get the ball into the other team's goal. You can use any body part except your hands or arms. Only the goalie, the person guarding the goal, can use his or her hands. The game can be played quickly. It's a friendly game of action and skill.

Nations around the world take great pride in their soccer teams. When watching the World Cup, fans cheer. They jump and clap for their favorite teams. Soccer matches are a great way for the world to relax together. The world comes together for a very important reason: to have fun!

Use the words to complete the sentences below.

skill   tournament   cheer   soccer   billion   goalie

1. The most popular sport in the world is _____ .

2. World Cup is a soccer _____ that happens every four years.

3. The 2014 World Cup final was watched by about one _____ people around the world.

4. In soccer, the only person who can use hands is the _____ .

5. People who play soccer in the World Cup have great _____ .

6. Fans _____ for their favorite team.

Danger! Animal Alert

When an animal becomes extinct, it is gone from Earth forever. Humans can do nothing to bring the animal back. But animals that are endangered still have a chance to survive. Humans have worked hard to keep track of endangered plants and animals. Right now, there are more than 16,900 plants and animals that are in danger of disappearing forever. Some are in much more trouble than others. Let's take a look at three of the most endangered animals in the world.

Ivory-Billed Woodpecker

This bird may already be extinct. The last known sighting of the ivory-billed woodpecker was in Arkansas in 2004. Sightings after that point could not be confirmed.

There are still many woodpeckers around the world. However, this species has nearly died out. What's the reason? The bird lost its home when forests were cut down in the 1800s and 1900s. The animal could not thrive after that point. Hunters also played a part in making the bird an endangered species.

Northern Sportive Lemur

This cute little mammal lives in a tiny part of northern Madagascar. Madagascar still has many lemurs. However, the northern sportive lemur is nearly extinct. Some think there are only about 20 of the animal left. Just like the ivory-billed woodpecker, this animal's home was destroyed. Many of the lemurs were killed by hunters, too. But there may still be time to help. Education is our best hope. It's up to people to save this tiny, tree-loving animal.

Amur Leopard

This wild cat loves the cold weather. But only about 40 Amur leopards are left on Earth. They are tucked away in the far eastern portion of Russia. They are the only leopards in the world to live in such a cold place. Hunters pursue them for their beautiful spotted fur.

The public must help save endangered animals. Saving an endangered animal's home and preventing people from hunting it can mean saving its life.

Answer the questions below.

1. Why do scientists think the ivory-billed woodpecker could already be extinct?

_____

2. What caused the ivory-billed woodpecker to become endangered?

_____

3. About how many northern sportive lemurs are left, and where do they live?

_____

4. Why are northern sportive lemurs becoming extinct?

_____

5. About how many Amur leopards are left, and where do they live?

_____

6. What is the difference between an extinct animal and an endangered one?

_____

_____

Hurricane!

A hurricane is a giant, swirling, dangerous storm. In some areas of the world, the storm is called a cyclone. No matter what it's called, it is something that people must prepare for. Hurricanes can be very dangerous. Hurricane winds are faster than a speeding car. Buildings can be destroyed. Floods can occur.

So what causes these dangerous storms? Hurricanes begin over ocean waters that have become very warm. When the air above the ocean cools quickly, the warm air rises fast. A storm begins. Then hot air rises above the storm. Storm clouds start blowing in a circular motion. If all of the conditions are right, the storm can get stronger and stronger. When this happens, it is called a tropical storm.

Tropical storms can grow and speed up even more. They also move as they grow. When a tropical storm reaches wind speeds above 75 miles (121 km) per hour, it is known as a hurricane.

The strongest hurricanes can reach up to 200 miles (322 km) per hour. Some hurricanes are up to 600 miles (966 km) from end to end. A hurricane takes time to grow. A hurricane can last for up to a week before it calms down. Warm ocean waters below the storm keep making it stronger. When hurricanes reach land, they often end quickly. That's because the warm ocean waters are no longer giving them energy.

Although hurricanes can cause a lot of damage, there is often a lot of warning before hurricanes hit land. People have time to leave the area. They may board up windows. They may secure things that can fly around in the wind. They may have time to make the area safe before strong winds hit. This can save lives. The more we learn about hurricanes, the easier it can be to stay safe from them!

Read each question and circle the correct answer. Then answer the questions below.

1. In some other parts of the world, a hurricane is called a _____ .

   a) tropical storm   b) cyclone   c) tornado   d) strong storm

2. A hurricane forms over _____ .

   a) warm ocean waters   b) cold ocean waters

   c) areas of warm land   d) cold mountain areas

3. A tropical storm becomes a hurricane if it _____ .

   a) becomes 600 miles (966 km) wide

   b) reaches land

   c) has wind speeds over 75 miles (121 km) per hour

   d) all of the above

4. Why do hurricanes end more quickly once they go over land?

   a) It always takes a long time for a hurricane to reach land.

   b) The storm is no longer in a tropical area.

   c) There are trees that cause the storm to slow down.

   d) There is no longer warm ocean water giving the storm energy.

5. Why are hurricanes so dangerous?

   _____

6. What can people do to stay safe during a hurricane?

   _____

   _____

To the Moon!

"That's one small step for man, one giant leap for mankind." Those were the words spoken by astronaut Neil Armstrong. He said this as he stepped where no human had stepped before: on the moon. On July 20, 1969, the United States made history. The first mission to land on the moon was a success.

Today we may think that an astronaut in space is not such big news. After all, astronauts are in space every day. They spend time at the International Space Station. They repair tools that are used by researchers.

But in 1969, travel to the moon was a brand new idea. In fact, it had been only eight years since the first person had ever been in space. In 1961, Russian Yuri Gagarin spent 108 minutes orbiting Earth in a spacecraft. After that, Americans were determined to reach the moon.

And that's exactly what they did. After much training, three astronauts boarded the Apollo 11 spacecraft at Florida's Kennedy Space Center. Neil Armstrong and Buzz Aldrin would land on the moon. Michael Collins would stay in another vehicle. It was called the command module. Collins would make sure the other astronauts returned to the ship safely.

Half a billion people watched the landing on TV. There was a lot to worry about, but the landing went well. The event was like nothing anyone had seen before. The three men returned to Earth safely.

The moon mission prompted many other trips to space. Americans landed on the moon five more times. The mark of Armstrong's boot is still on the dusty moon surface. An American flag still stands on the moon. That giant leap for mankind was just the first step of our space exploration.

What's the order? Write *1, 2, 3, 4, 5, 6* on the lines.

_____ People turned on their televisions to watch the moon landing.

_____ Astronauts returned to Earth safely from the moon.

_____ Neil Armstrong was the first person on the moon.

_____ The Apollo 11 spacecraft was built to travel to the moon.

_____ Astronauts left an American flag on the moon.

_____ Russian Yuri Gagarin orbited Earth.

The Candy Man

You might think that someone who decides to make candy for a living would be an instant success! But that's not exactly what happened to one candy maker. Milton Hershey had a couple of failed candy businesses before he made it big.

But sometimes success is worth the wait. Now when you say the name Hershey, you think of the famous candy bar or chocolate kisses. But did you know that Hershey started out by making caramels? He learned the candy trade as a teen in Lancaster, Pennsylvania.

Success came slowly for Hershey. His first couple of attempts to start candy businesses failed. Then he started the Lancaster Caramel Company. They shipped caramels all over the United States. Hershey had customers halfway around the world. He hired 1,400 people to work for his business. There was a lot of money to be made in candy!

Hershey first started making chocolate so he could add a sweet coating to his caramels. But people were interested in the chocolate as much as the caramels. Soon, Hershey opened the Hershey Chocolate Company. Hershey worked for years on getting just the right mixture of milk, sugar, and cocoa to make his chocolate bars a hit.

In 1900, Hershey was ready to make his business huge! He opened a factory in Pennsylvania. By 1905, he needed an even bigger factory. This one was near ports so he could get deliveries of sugar and cocoa. It was near dairy farms so he could get the freshest milk.

An entire town was built around the factory. The town had stores and a meeting hall. It had a swimming pool and schools. It even had an amusement park. What is the name of the town? Hershey, Pennsylvania! To this day, the town remains one of Pennsylvania's favorite tourist attractions.

Read each statement. Write *true* or *false*.

1. Milton Hershey failed at candy businesses
   a few times before he succeeded. _____

2. Hershey started out making
   caramels, not chocolate. _____

3. Hershey started making chocolate because
   people asked for chocolate bars. _____

4. The Hershey Company has been using the same mixture
   of milk, sugar, and cocoa since its first chocolate bar. _____

5. Hershey opened a factory near
   dairy farms and a shipping port. _____

6. People still visit Hershey's factory
   town in Pennsylvania today. _____

All About Diamonds

When you hear the word "diamond," do you think of fine jewels? Or do you think of drills or huge machines in factories? Diamonds are used for both!

We know that diamonds are beautiful in jewelry. They sparkle in the light. People spend a lot of money on diamonds, too. In the United States, people spend $18 billion each year on diamonds to be used in jewelry. But diamonds are more than just pretty things to wear.

The word "diamond" comes from the Greek word meaning "unbreakable." And that's what diamonds are. They are the world's hardest known natural material. That's why they are so useful in industry. They can cut through almost any material. They can stand up to very high heat. Diamonds are used at the tips of drills to cut through hard surfaces. They can even cut through rock.

Diamonds form deep underground. They form in a very hot part of Earth called the mantle. Intense pressure and heat help form these amazing minerals. Diamonds come to the surface through volcanic activity. They are then mined, or dug from the ground. The very first diamonds were found in India. Today, most diamonds are from Botswana, Russia, and Canada.

Some diamonds have landed on Earth in meteorites. That means that diamonds are found in space. The areas around Saturn and Jupiter are studded with diamonds!

Answer the questions below.

1. What are some words that can describe diamonds?

_____

2. What are some ways people use diamonds?

_____

3. How did diamonds get their name?

_____

4. How are diamonds formed?

_____

5. How do people remove diamonds from the Earth?

_____

6. How can diamonds come to Earth from outer space?

_____

The *Titanic*

It was once called an unsinkable ship. It was also called the Ship of Dreams. The RMS *Titanic* was built to be the most impressive ship in the world. It was a luxury cruise liner. On its first voyage in 1912, it carried some of the richest passengers in the world. More than 100,000 people watched as the ship sailed off on its first voyage. Little did they know that the ship would not return.

On the fifth night of the voyage, things were going as planned. A crew member was on the lookout for sheets of ice and icebergs in the cold waters. Suddenly, the lookout, Frederick Fleet, spotted trouble. "Iceberg, straight ahead!" he yelled. Because of the communication systems at the time, it took about 37 seconds before the ship began to turn. It was too late. The crew did all they could to save the ship. But after several hours, the unsinkable ship was on its way to the bottom of the ocean.

Many people escaped in lifeboats. But even more did not survive. The ship disappeared into the ocean without a trace until 1985. At that time it was found by a crew of ocean explorers. The crews used cameras and sonar to help find the sunken ship. It was 12,467 feet (3,800 m) below the surface of the ocean. New technologies allowed crews to find objects that were lost on the ship. Some were brought up as lasting memories of the voyage. Now, more than 100 years after the *Titanic* sank, some of the artifacts are on display for people to view. The tragic voyage fascinates a new generation of people.

Use the words to complete the sentences below.

communication   iceberg   unsinkable

technologies   cameras   sink

1. Before sailing, the RMS *Titanic* was called an _____ ship.

2. During its first voyage, the giant cruise liner hit an _____ .

3. The ship could not turn right away because of slow

_____ .

4. After it took about 37 seconds to turn, the RMS *Titanic* began to

_____ .

5. Many years later, scientists used _____ to find the ship.

6. Today we have found some of the items from the ship because
   we used new _____ .

To the Top!

Some people crave adventure. They want to be the first person to break a record. They want to do something nobody has ever done before. In the first half of the 1900s, people competed to be the first to climb the world's tallest mountain. Mount Everest is a 29,035-foot (8,850 m) mountain in the Himalayas. The mountain lies between China's Tibet and the country of Nepal.

The trek up the mountain is very dangerous. Hikers must be prepared with the right supplies. Food must be brought. Clothes must be warm enough to survive in the freezing temperatures. The air at the top of the mountain is very thin. There is not as much oxygen as at ground level. People have trouble breathing on such a high mountain. They bring tanks of oxygen with them for breathing.

Many people tried to climb Mount Everest and did not survive. Then, on May 29, 1953, the first humans in history saw the top of the mountain. Edmund Hillary from New Zealand reached the top. With him was Tenzing Norgay from Nepal. The men had done the almost impossible. After only 15 minutes at the top, they started to climb back down. They were dangerously low on oxygen.

Today many people have climbed to the top of the mountain. They can do so in part because of the good work of Hillary and Norgay. On their carefully planned trip, the men set up nine camps. Some of these camps, or resting spots, are still used today by climbers. The way the mountain is climbed is very important. The time of day that climbers set out on their hikes is important. They must rest a lot to get their bodies used to the changes in the air. It can take weeks to make the trip. The long journey is worth it for many climbers, however. They get a rare view from the top of the world.

Circle the best word or phrase to complete each sentence.

1. The first humans reached the top of Mount Everest in _____ .

   1900   **1953**

2. The climbers were Tenzing Norgay from Nepal and Edmund Hillary from _____.

   Great Britain   **New Zealand**

3. The men spent a very short time at the top of the mountain because they were low on _____.

   food   **oxygen**

4. Today, climbers use the same _____ as Hillary and Norgay.

   camps   **tents**

5. While climbing Mount Everest, hikers must get used to the changes in the _____.

   air and temperature   **light and season**

6. Climbing to the top of Mount Everest is a _____ hiking experience.

   beginner's   **dangerous**

Monticello

Thomas Jefferson was a Founding Father and the third president of the United States. He was a true American. But he knew about more than just politics. He also knew a lot about building. He learned by reading books about architecture. That was enough for him to design and start building his own home on a beautiful hill in Virginia. He called the building Monticello, which is Italian for "little mountain."

Building this home took decades. Jefferson started the work as a young man. However, there were many interruptions. First, the American Revolution kept him from his plans. Then his career got in the way. After his wife, Martha, died, Jefferson moved to France to be an ambassador until 1789. When he saw the architecture in Paris, he was inspired again. He returned to Virginia with new plans for his home. He added features he had seen in France. He added the building's famous octagonal dome. It was the first one in the United States.

When the building was finished, it was double the size of his original plans. There are beautiful gardens on the grounds. The home holds Jefferson's huge book and art collections. It also showcases some of Jefferson's inventions. These include a spinning bookstand, a sundial, and a copy machine.

Today, people can visit Monticello. The columns and domed roof make the building easy to recognize. It shows how the United States is a mix of ideas from different nations and cultures. The building is an example of true American architecture. Monticello was made by a true American.

Read each question and circle the correct answer. Then answer the questions below.

1. What does the name Monticello mean?

   a) strong leader   **b)** little mountain

   c) new nation   **d)** Italian home

2. What events kept Jefferson from completing the building of Monticello?

   a) the American Revolution

   b) Jefferson's time as an ambassador

   c) Jefferson's time in Paris

   d) all of the above

3. By the time Jefferson finished Monticello, the plans had _____ .

   a) doubled in size

   b) tripled in size

   c) become much smaller

   d) stayed as he had always planned

4. Monticello has building ideas that Jefferson thought of in _____ .

   a) Washington, DC   **b)** France

   c) Italy   **d)** Spain

5. Why does the author say that Monticello is an example of true American architecture?

   _____

6. Why does the author say that Jefferson is a true American?

   _____

Superfood: Apple

What's good about an apple? Plenty! Have you ever heard that an apple a day keeps the doctor away? All of the nutrients in apples will help keep you healthy.

You can get some of the vitamin C you need by eating one of these red, green, or yellow fruits. Vitamin C helps prevent colds and other illnesses. It also helps your body to get better faster once you are sick.

Apples also help keep blood sugar under control. There's a sugar in your blood called glucose. Eating apples can keep the levels of glucose in your body at a good level. This means your energy levels will stay under control. Apples also keep your heart healthy. They reduce the risk of some cancers. There's a lot to like about an apple!

Another great benefit of the apple is that it gets rid of hunger. Studies have shown that you can stay fuller longer if you eat an apple in its whole form. Applesauce and apple juice do not keep people full as long.

Apples are good for you, no matter what kind you choose. Some are sweet. Others are tart. Growers have combined so many different types of apples that there are more than 7,000 kinds. Each one is great for keeping our bodies healthy. So enjoy whichever type of apple is your favorite!

Circle the best word or phrase to complete each sentence.

1. Apples have a lot of _____.

   vitamin C   vitamin D

2. The nutrients in apples help keep people from getting _____.

   headaches   colds

3. Apples also keep levels of _____ under control.

   oxygen   blood sugar

4. Apples can also help prevent heart problems and _____.

   cancer   chicken pox

5. If you eat whole apples instead
   of applesauce, you may feel _____ longer.

   hungry   full

6. Apples can be red, green, or _____.

   yellow   blue

The World's Oldest Tree

Imagine having more than 9,550 birthdays! There's a tree on Earth that has been around for that many years. The oldest living tree on Earth began growing its roots at the end of the last ice age. Scientists discovered the tree in Sweden in 2004. There's nothing unusual about the tree itself. The tree is a Norwegian spruce. This is a common tree that people use in their homes to decorate for Christmas.

How did this tree live so long? It's the roots of the tree that date back so many thousands of years. The stem and trunk of the tree live around 600 years. That's also a long time for a tree. But after they die, new stems and trunks grow from the old roots. A new section of the tree may live another 600 years. This cycle can continue again and again. Scientists have found other spruce trees in Sweden. Some of these are close to 6,000 years old!

The 9,550-year old Norway spruce lives on a mountain. Low shrubs grow all around it. The area where the tree was found gave scientists some details about Earth's past. Before the tree was found, they thought that spruce trees only started growing in that part of the world 2,000 years ago. Now they know the trees lived in the area closer to 10,000 years ago! They know that the area also could not have trees much older than this spruce. About 11,000 years ago, the area was covered in ice from the last ice age.

Trees as old as this Norway spruce can teach us a lot about Earth's past. They also show us a lot about the life cycle of some plants. This one is a survivor!

Answer the questions below.

1. How old is the world's oldest tree?

_____

2. What is the oldest part of the tree?

_____

3. How does the tree grow for so many years?

_____

4. Where does the oldest tree live?

_____

5. What did the discovery of the spruce teach scientists about that area of the world?

_____

6. What was happening on Earth at the time the oldest spruce first began to grow?

_____

Favorite Fairy Tales

You know the stories well: "Little Red Riding Hood," "Sleeping Beauty," "Puss in Boots," and "Cinderella." You may have read the tales. You may have seen them made into movies. But who came up with these classics? A man named Charles Perrault wrote all four of these famous stories. Today, however, the writer is not nearly as famous as his popular stories.

Perrault lived during the 1600s in France. He was a well-known scholar. Perrault did not think the great thinkers of his time would be interested in stories for children. So he published the stories under the name of his son, Pierre. He called the collection *Tales of Mother Goose.*

The stories became famous. They were well loved by people around the world. They became bedtime stories. They were translated into many languages. The stories are still loved today.

Perrault was not the only person to write clever stories for young children. During the early 1800s, two brothers from Germany called themselves the Brothers Grimm. They wrote some tales you may find familiar. They wrote "Snow White," "Hansel and Gretel," and "Rapunzel."

Also in the 1800s, Hans Christian Andersen became known for his fairy tales. The poet wrote favorites such as "The Little Mermaid," "The Ugly Duckling," and "The Snow Queen."

The next time you read one of the old classics, think about the authors. Each one was written by a superstar writer of his time. Their stories have lasted generations. They have been translated into many languages. They have been retold to children for hundreds of years. And they will likely be told to children for hundreds of years into the future.

Read each question and circle the correct answer. Then answer the questions below.

1. Which author wrote the children's classic "Cinderella"?

    a) the Brothers Grimm   **b)** Hans Christian Andersen

    c) Charles Perrault   **d)** Shakespeare

2. What country were the Brothers Grimm from?

    a) France   **b)** Germany   **c)** England   **d)** Scotland

3. Which classic story did author Hans Christian Andersen write?

    a) "Sleeping Beauty"   **b)** "Rapunzel"

    c) "The Little Mermaid"   **d)** "Little Red Riding Hood"

4. Which classic story did the Brothers Grimm write?

    a) "Sleeping Beauty"   **b)** "Snow White"

    c) "The Little Mermaid"   **d)** "Little Red Riding Hood"

5. Why did Charles Perrault publish *Tales of Mother Goose* under his son's name?

    _____

6. How are children around the world able to read the same stories?

    _____

Helen Keller

Imagine a world in which you could not see or hear. When Helen Keller was very young, she became ill. The sickness caused her to lose both her hearing and her sight. She was in a silent world of darkness. The little girl from Alabama suffered. For years, she could not communicate. She became frustrated and angry.

When Helen was 7, her parents knew she needed help. A tutor named Anne Sullivan came to help Helen learn to communicate. Anne and Helen were a good match. In just a month, Helen was learning sign language. This is a special language that deaf people use. They speak or spell with signs formed with their hands.

Since Helen had not spoken or heard words since she was a baby, she also had to learn what words meant. It was an incredible challenge. Anne had to teach Helen sign language and teach her words at the same time. Luckily, Anne was a great teacher. When she spelled out the word "water," she placed Helen's hand under water. Helen knew right away what the word meant. Next, they did the same with the word "ground." Helen began learning words very quickly. She was inspired to learn!

Helen spent years learning to speak, write, and understand people. She learned different languages. She learned a special language called Braille. It allows blind people to read books. Raised dots are arranged as letters and words. The reader uses fingers to feel the letters instead of eyes to see them.

Helen wrote the story of her life. She then wrote ten more books and many articles. Her work helped make people aware of her struggle. People discovered how deaf and blind people learn. She taught people about the challenges of being without sight and hearing. Helen came a long way out of her childhood world of silent darkness. As an adult, she inspired and taught many people.

Answer the questions below.

1. How did Helen Keller become deaf and blind?

_____

2. How did Helen's parents help her to start learning to communicate?

_____

3. Why did Helen have to learn both sign language and the names for things?

_____

4. What is Braille?

_____

5. Why did Helen have to learn Braille?

_____

6. Why were so many people inspired by Helen Keller?

_____

How Big Is the Solar System?

One night, look out into space from Earth. You'll see stars and the moon. If you are lucky, you can catch a glimpse of a planet. Any planet viewed from Earth would look like a tiny speck of dust. When we view things from far away, they look tiny.

So how large are planets? Each planet is a very different size from the others. It can be confusing to think about which planet is the largest and which is the smallest. The planets are so big that it's hard to get a good idea about their relative size.

The chart below will help you understand how big the planets are compared to the sun. Think of the sun as the size of a kickball eight inches across. The planets would be tiny compared to this ball.

IF THE SUN WERE AN EIGHT-INCH BALL:	
Mercury would be the size of a...	poppy seed.
Venus would be the size of a...	pea.
Earth would be the size of a...	pea.
Mars would be the size of a...	poppy seed.
Jupiter would be the size of a...	walnut.
Saturn would be the size of an...	acorn.
Uranus would be the size of a...	peanut.
Neptune would be the size of a...	peanut.

If the solar system were this small, the distance between the planets would be just a few steps from each other. If these tiny seeds and nuts were to travel around the kickball, they would give a sense of how huge the real solar system is.

Read each statement. Write *true* or *false*.

1. Space is so large that it is hard to
   understand how large objects in space are. _____

2. If the Sun were an eight-inch ball,
   Earth would be the size of a poppy seed. _____

3. If the Sun were an eight-inch ball,
   Saturn would be the size of an acorn. _____

4. Jupiter is the largest object in the solar system. _____

5. Mercury is larger than Earth. _____

6. Jupiter is larger than Neptune. _____

How to Write a Persuasive Letter

Have you ever felt strongly about something and wanted everyone to know about it? Maybe you wanted to complain about something that was unfair. Maybe you wanted to get people to do or think something. These are all perfect times to write a persuasive letter.

A persuasive letter should get a reader to think or act in a certain way. Suppose a store sold you a ripped shirt. You did not notice the tear until you got home. Then the store would not give you your money back. You could write a letter! Your letter would try to get the store owner to understand your point of view.

First, decide whom to write to and why. Then start your letter by stating why you are writing it. Perhaps start with something such as, "On May 11, I was sold a shirt that had a big rip in the sleeve. I tried to return it, but I was not given my money back. I am writing to try to get my money returned to me."

A persuasive letter should be formal. You want the reader to understand that you are serious and that your idea is important. Then you must give solid reasons why the person should do or think what you want them to. List the most important ideas first. Give examples if you can. This will help the reader to see things your way.

Then think about why the person might say no to your idea. Come up with an answer for that idea. For example, the owner of the store may say that they do not accept returns. Have your answer ready. For example, "Although you say you do not accept returns, this item was damaged. It should not have been sold in the first place."

Summarize your main points at the end of your letter. Then wait for a response.

Write *1, 2, 3, 4, 5, 6* on the lines to show the steps in writing a persuasive letter.

_____ Tell why you are right and that the reader should agree with you.

_____ Decide whom you will be writing to and why.

_____ Think about how the reader might argue with you.

_____ Summarize your main points at the end of the letter.

_____ Write your reason for writing the letter.

_____ Explain why the reader's argument is wrong.

The Fastest Mammal

What mammal can go from a resting position to 60 miles (97 km) per hour in just three seconds? It's the cheetah! This quick cat can outrun any other animal. That's what makes it such a deadly hunter.

And the cheetah doesn't just run around at top speeds looking for food. It uses its great eyesight to find prey. When it knows exactly where it is headed, it bolts into action. The animal can even make sharp, sudden turns very quickly. Cheetahs like to catch antelopes and hares. But all animals in the cheetah's African grassland habitat are on the lookout for this quick and clever cat.

Cheetahs are sometimes confused with leopards. Both animals have spotted fur. But cheetahs are smaller, with flat heads that are different than the leopard. Cheetahs also have black marks that look like tear stains under their eyes.

This amazing animal can grow to be up to 140 pounds (64 kg) and 4.5 feet (1.4 m) long. It is hard to believe, but cheetahs only need to drink water every three or four days.

Cheetahs live up to 12 years. A mother cheetah will have about three cubs at a time. She will spend about 18 months teaching and feeding them. Then they are ready to live on their own.

Because of human activity, cheetah habitats are being destroyed. Scientists think only about 10,000 are left in the world. This means the animal could soon become endangered. Hopefully humans can help to keep this speedy animal roaming the plains of Africa!

Circle the best word or phrase to complete each sentence.

1. A cheetah can run up to 60 _____ per hour.

   kilometers   **miles**

2. The cheetah also uses its great sense of _____ to find prey to chase.

   smell   **sight**

3. Cheetahs live in _____ environments.

   desert   **grassland**

4. Every three or four days, cheetahs will need _____ .

   water   **sleep**

5. Cheetahs live in _____ .

   Africa   **North America**

6. Scientists think cheetahs may soon become _____ .

   extinct   **endangered**

Answer Key

Page 5
1. true
2. false
3. false
4. true
5. true
6. false

Page 7
1. vitamin C; potassium; fiber
2. Strawberries can help you avoid getting colds and diseases such as heart disease and cancer.
3. Potassium helps muscles work and stay strong and helps blood flow well.
4. Strawberries can be eaten raw, in muffins, or in snack bars.
5. A superfood is a food with vitamins and nutrients that is especially good for the body.
6. Answers will vary.

Page 9
1. c
2. d
3. b
4. a
5. Answers will vary but may include: The team passes the ball over the opposite team's goal line and gets the ball past the goalie.
6. They have a face-off.

Page 11
1. camel
2. South America; Andes
3. 75; 20
4. It will get angry and refuse to move.
5. They are good at carrying goods long distances. They do not need much water. They can eat a wide variety of plants and grasses.
6. Answers will vary.

Page 13
1. 3
   5
   1
   4
   2
2. Answers will vary but may include: Today, games look much better and can be played at home and carried around as portable systems. In the past, the games did not look as good. They had to be shared at arcades and played by paying quarters.

Page 15
1. there is no gravity
2. eat; sleep
3. spoil
4. rehydrated
5. the person will float around and cannot rest
6. are strapped against a wall to stay in one place

Page 17
1. true
2. false
3. true
4. false
5. false
6. false

Page 19
1. Possible answers include: They cannot fly. They live in very cold temperatures. The mother leaves the egg while the father keeps it warm. They dive 2,000 feet. They stay underwater for 20 minutes.
2. They huddle in a group and take turns moving to the outside of the huddle.
3. The male keeps the egg warm.
4. The female keeps it in a warm pouch.
5. Penguins eat fish.
6. They get fish by diving deep and staying underwater for up to 20 minutes.

Page 21
4
1
6
2
5
3

Page 23
1. mountains
2. Italy
3. 24 hours
4. ash
5. centuries
6. hardened

Page 25
1. c
2. a
3. e
4. b
5. d
6. Answers will vary but may include: When dragonflies are young, they are nymphs and do not have wings. They grow their wings later after they go through a metamorphosis.

Page 27
Answers will vary but may include:
1. If the camera does not have an automatic focus, the photographer will have to do the focusing so the picture comes out clear.
2. The flash creates light so the subject can be seen.
3. Most flashes only work up to about ten feet, so the subject may not be in that area.
4. The photographer should think about what to get in the frame, and whether to hold the camera sideways to frame the picture better.
5. Answers will vary.

Page 29
1. opinion
2. opinion
3. fact
4. fact
5. fact
6. opinion

Page 31
1. b
2. d
3. b
4. c
5. Her last messages were not heard.
6. She was the first female pilot to become well-known. She inspired women to reach for their goals.

Page 33
1. It is based on *harpaston*.
2. It was played 2,500 years ago.
3. Players had to stop the other team from getting a ball to the other team's goal.
4. They wanted people to play games that would help in war, such as fencing or archery.
5. In 1869, colleges began playing football against each other.
6. It is more popular in America than in other places.

Page 35
1. c
2. a
3. c
4. d
5. Dolphins have large brains and are very intelligent. They can perform tasks and remember things better than other animals.
6. The main idea is that dolphins are very smart.

Page 37
1. true
2. false
3. true
4. false
5. false
6. true

Page 39
1. crust
2. plates
3. quake
4. energy
5. strength
6. safe

Page 41

1. e
2. c
3. b
4. d
5. a
6. A mountain may form when two plates hit against each other and move over a long time, making one rise up high. A mountain may also form when a volcano erupts many times and lava hardens along the outside in the shape of a mountain.

Page 43

1. wild
2. 10,000
3. food
4. hunt
5. domesticated
6. 40

Page 45

2
5
4
1
6
3

Page 47

1. false
2. true
3. false
4. true
5. false
6. false

Page 49

1. It is on the border of the United States and Canada, in New York and Ontario.
2. Sheets of ice from the last ice age melted and moved, carving out rivers and the waterfall.
3. During the summer, 2,800 tons of water goes over Niagara Falls every second.
4. It is used for drinking, fishing, boating, swimming, and making power.
5. Some tourists have gone over the falls.
6. It is noisy because so much water is rushing down the waterfall.

Page 51

1. c
2. b
3. d
4. a
5. Recycling keeps trash out of landfills. It is good for the Earth.
6. Set up bins and mark what they are used for. Let people know what they can and cannot recycle. Get help from an adult to deliver the bins to a recycling plant.

Page 53

1. Mars is about 120 degrees Fahrenheit colder than Earth.
2. The atmosphere on Mars does not have protection from the sun's rays, so humans would get sunburned.
3. It is covered in red dust.
4. The dust would make it hard for a human to breathe.
5. A visitor to Mars would see red dust, volcanoes, and two moons.
6. Answers will vary.

Page 55

1. exercising
2. mood
3. oxygen
4. sleep
5. muscles
6. healthy

Page 57

1. false
2. false
3. true
4. false
5. true
6. true

Page 59

1. Video games used to look like blips of light and now they look as real as a movie.
2. They may be placed over the eyes so the player can see the action happening around them.
3. The image comes out of the console and shows around the room instead of on a screen.
4. The player may be able to slide a finger in the air and move a switch without touching one.

5. Some ideas come from entertainment, such as movies or books.
6. Answers will vary.

Page 61

4
1
6
3
5
2

Page 63

1. soccer
2. tournament
3. billion
4. goalie
5. skill
6. cheer

Page 65

1. It has not been officially spotted since 2004.
2. Its forest home was lost and it was hunted.
3. There are about 20 left, and they live in northern Madagascar.
4. The lemurs' home was destroyed, and many were hunted.
5. There are about 40 left, and they live in the far eastern portion of Russia.
6. An extinct animal is gone forever, and an endangered one is in danger of disappearing.

Page 67

1. b
2. a
3. c
4. d
5. Strong winds and flooding can cause damage and create dangerous conditions.
6. People can board up windows, secure items that can fly around in the wind, and get out of the area until the storm is over.

Page 69

3
6
4
2
5
1

Page 71

1. true
2. true
3. false
4. false
5. true
6. true

Page 73

1. sparkly, pretty, strong, unbreakable
2. People use diamonds as jewelry and in industry tools such as drills.
3. Diamonds were named for the Greek word for "unbreakable."
4. They form deep underground in Earth's mantle, under a lot of heat and pressure.
5. Diamonds are mined from Earth after they are brought to the crust by volcanic activity.
6. Some diamonds come to Earth in meteorites.

Page 75

1. unsinkable
2. iceberg
3. communication
4. sink
5. cameras
6. technologies

Page 77

1. 1953
2. New Zealand
3. oxygen
4. camps
5. air and temperature
6. dangerous

Page 79

1. b
2. d
3. a
4. b
5. America is a mix of different ideas from different cultures, and that's what Monticello is.
6. Jefferson was one of the founders of the nation and one of the first presidents.

Page 81

1. vitamin C
2. colds
3. blood sugar
4. cancer
5. full
6. yellow

Page 83

1. The oldest tree is 9,550 years old.
2. The roots are the oldest part of the tree.
3. The stem and trunk grow for about 600 years, then new ones grow in their place again and again.
4. The tree lives on a mountain in Sweden.
5. They learned that the spruce tree has been living in that area of the world for nearly 10,000 years, not 2,000 years as they first thought.
6. The tree began growing as the last ice age was ending.

Page 85

1. c
2. b
3. c
4. b
5. He was a scholar and he did not think others would be interested in children's stories.
6. These fairy tales have been translated into many languages.

Page 87

1. She had an illness as a child that caused her to lose her hearing and sight.
2. They found Helen a tutor named Anne Sullivan.
3. She was very young when she lost her hearing, so she also had to learn the names for words and ideas like a baby would.
4. Braille is a way to write words for blind people so they can read books. Raised dots are felt with their fingers and form letters and words.
5. Helen learned Braille so she could read books.
6. People saw all the challenges she overcame. She made people aware of the challenges that blind and deaf people face every day.

Page 89

1. true
2. false
3. true
4. false
5. false
6. true

Page 91

3
1
4
6
2
5

Page 93

1. miles
2. sight
3. grassland
4. water
5. Africa
6. endangered

Image Credits